Circus World Museum
presents

SHOW TRAINS
OF THE 20TH CENTURY

Fred Dahlinger, Jr.

Iconografix

Iconografix, Inc.
PO Box 446
Hudson, Wisconsin 54016 USA

Library of Congress Card Number: 00-132393

ISBN 1-58388-030-5

00 01 02 03 04 05 06 5 4 3 2 1

Printed in the United States of America

Cover and book design by Shawn Glidden

Copy Editing by Dylan Frautschi

Book Proposals

Iconografix is a publishing company specializing in books for transportation enthusiasts. We publish in a number of different areas, including Automobiles, Auto Racing, Buses, Construction Equipment, Emergency Equipment, Farming Equipment, Railroads & Trucks. The Iconografix imprint is constantly growing and expanding into new subject areas.

Authors, editors, and knowledgeable enthusiasts in the field of transportation history are invited to contact the Editorial Department at Iconografix, Inc., PO Box 446, Hudson, WI 54016.

INTRODUCTION

From the 1850s until today, the railroads of America have hauled privately owned show cars and trains that brought amusement, entertainment, and education to millions of Americans. The railroad was the means by which nearly all goods and people were moved from one community to another in the first half of the century. Shows, seeking to reach those same people, traveled via those same tracks. With our overwhelming dependence upon roadway vehicles and airplanes today, it is difficult to comprehend the importance of the railroads to show commerce in the 20th century.

This book contains three areas of show train coverage. The first portion chronicles wild west show trains. It and the next section, covering a variety of show operations, stretch the range of the book title back to the late nineteenth century. One could not understand the subject matter by simply commencing in 1901. The final portion of the book covers carnival trains, an industry that recently experienced, without any celebratory fanfare whatever, its 100th year of existence.

The array of photographs attempts to satisfy the curiosity and learning desires of many different perspectives. By design, the coverage includes action shots, builders' photos, views that illustrate specific points and others that are simply great photography. The illustrations herein are generally in chronological order within each of the sections to provide continuity, but there are exceptions. As with all show train topics, the body of photographic documentation is limited.

The circus was the first and largest user of the railroads for transport. It was the circus, minimally in the 1850s, and then in a big way in the 1870s, that launched a movement toward private show ownership of specialized railroad cars. Circus managers developed the techniques for advertising shows that moved nationwide. They also devised the logistical technology that made rapid movement of field shows possible. The same techniques and methodologies were adopted when the first wild west show trains and carnival trains entered service in the 1880s and 1890s.

Shows utilized wood frame cars from the 1870s until the late 1920s. There was a lively trade in second hand cars, enabling wild west operations and carnivals to acquire used cars at a fraction of the cost of new vehicles. Given its early entrance into railroad show operations, the circus business frequently became a supplier of second hand cars for other field shows. Traveling shows also bought new vehicles from the same builders that fabricated circus cars. The Barney & Smith Car Company and the Mt. Vernon Car Manufacturing Company were two of the leading suppliers. For shows with limited capital, wood flats and stocks could be leased from the Venice Transportation Company and the Arms Palace Horse Car Company and the Burton Stock Car Company, among others. Cars to house and transport people were acquired from system railroads, the Pullman Company or second hand dealers, including the Southern Iron & Equipment Company and Fitz-Hugh & Company.

Though the P. T. Barnum circus had some unusual metal frame flat cars made of tubing or pipe in 1876, the first conventional steel show cars were made for a wild west outfit and a carnival in 1911. A few carnivals invested immediately in steel cars, but nearly all shows delayed their conversions until forced to do so by railroads in the 1920s. Builders of steel show cars included the Standard Steel Car Company, Haffner-Thrall Car Company, Warren Tank Car Company and Mt. Vernon. Carnivals appear to have favored the Warren firm with the majority of their steel car orders. Steel cars that were fabricated from the 1910s through the 1930s served until the 1950s. One flat car remains in show service today. The depletion of the pool of usable steel cars in the late 1940s and early 1950s brought about a limited amount of specialized car building activity. Subsequently, newer show cars have been adapted system cars.

Shows in the 1880s and 1890s journeyed on cars that varied from about 45 to 60 feet long, with capacities ranging from 20 to 40 tons. The first steel cars of 1911 had a 40-ton rating. Seventy-foot cars may have been made by 1914, for certain by 1920, and the 72-foot cars about 1928. The 50-ton capacity plateau was reached by 1927.

Buffalo Bill's Wild West traveled by rail for the first time in 1884. It is thought that the outfit leased cars from system railroads or car rental firms. Following a partnership agreement signed with circus magnate James A. Bailey a decade later, the show went forth on former circus cars furnished by Bailey as one part of his contractual responsibility. The first wild west proprietor to travel on his own cars was probably Gordon W. Lillie, better known as "Pawnee Bill." Lillie commanded a wild west operation that was second only to the renowned Cody outfit. Shortly after the turn of the century he quit leasing cars from the railroads and purchased his own train of show cars.

Cody and Lillie dominated the wild west field until the Miller Bros. and Edward Arlington entered the business with their 101 Ranch Real Wild West in 1908. In the early 1910s there was a burst of wild west show activity that lasted until the eve of World War I. The genre then died out until the Millers resurrected it in 1925. Movie idol Buck Jones fielded a railroad show in 1929 and Col. Tim McCoy did the same in 1938, but all three became victims of the Depression. A wild west show has not traveled by rails since.

Throughout the last half of the nineteenth century and the first half of the twentieth century, numerous showmen utilized purchased or leased cars to transport their attractions. Hall shows commenced to move by rail quite early, in the 1860s, as did the first whale shows, about 1881. Theater troupes, dime museums, aquariums, minstrel shows, theater troupes and other forms of entertainment all found it convenient to move by rail from one venue to another. Frankly, there were no alternatives unless one showed along the inland rivers or the seacoasts and moved by boat.

In some cases, such as museum, aquarium and zoo trains, the railroad cars actually housed the show. They were walk-through type exhibits wherein visitors entered at one end of the car, or cars, and gazed upon the features contained therein, exiting at the other end. In the case of minstrel, fighting the flames, Uncle Tom's Cabin and repertoire theater troupes, the cars hauled show apparatus that was erected on a show grounds or in a theater that had been hired or leased for show purposes.

Performers of all types traveled by train across the country. A few that became wealthy could afford their own private cars. Those that truly excelled may have had several cars to house and carry their personal belongings, show equipment, and in one case, their favorite horses and carriage. Some of the private cars were simply re-decorated system cars. Others were special built for show purposes, a few having elegantly applied paint decorations and scenic panels to advertise the show as it rolled to the next engagement.

The American carnival was an outgrowth of the midways at agricultural fairs and particularly the Midway Plaisance at the 1893 World's Columbian Exposition. Infused with ideas imported from English fairgrounds in the latter half of the 1890s, early carnival operations benefited from the burgeoning interest in street fairs to promote communities. Frank Gaskill of Alliance, Ohio, is generally credited with launching the first complete carnival that played an entire season, in 1898. The traveling midways provided a week or more of diversion in communities that wanted a street fair, lacked a local amusement park, or needed a money making attraction to bolster and provide entertainment at an agricultural fair. Originally the carnival midway consisted of a variety of shows under canvas tents, games of chance, concession stands, and a few mechanical rides. The shows became elaborate productions, in some cases fronted by huge carved facades that were gold-leafed. The number and variety of mechanical thrills proliferated, as did their size and cost. Games of skill or chance are often remembered in a scope of influence beyond their actual presence.

The carnival reached its zenith, in terms of importance and popularity, in the years immediately after the two World Wars. A new attraction, television, decimated outdoor show attendance with its novelty in the early 1950s. The big, tented shows quickly became a thing of the past. Games of chance were outlawed and midways were dominated by the rides, or "iron" as it's sometimes called in the business.

Many fine carnivals traveled by truck but the biggest and best shows from the early 1900s through the 1950s were mostly those that moved by special railroad trains. To the uneducated eye, they generally resembled circus trains, with stock and boxcars, flat cars loaded with wagons, and sleeping cars for their personnel. A few started as "gilly" operations that relied principally on manpower for loading and unloading. Flat car-type operations started early and readily embraced existing circus train technology. A number of shows grew into the 50-car class, but only one reached the enormous size of 90 cars. The Sedlmayr family's gigantic Royal American Shows, "World's Largest Midway," is still remembered by industry veterans and carnival enthusiasts as a wondrous sight to behold.

Royal American Shows moved towards modernization but failed to update its rail equipment. The end of train operations came in 1981. The James E. Strates Shows leased and then purchased piggyback trailer flats in the late 1960s, when they were economical. Thereby the Strates family continued to efficiently move their carnival by rail and achieved the unique status of being the only carnival to travel by train today. The difficulty of finding adequate sidetrack space convenient to the show grounds that it plays has become a very real challenge. How long it will remain a railer will depend upon the creativity of the Strates management and the dynamics of the railroad and fair business.

Several associates of the author graciously provided support during the preparation of this book. Special appreciation is extended to Ray W. Buhrmaster, Jim Caldwell, Robert S. MacDougall, Fred D. Pfening, Jr., Richard J. Reynolds III, and Howard C. Tibbals in that regard. Additional assistance came from Bill Cooker, Ron Goldfeder, Fred Heatley, Paul Horsman, William F. Howes, Jr., Jim Parker, Fred D. Pfening III, Laura Sedlmayr, Dan Waldron, Byron R. West and others. I would also like to express thanks to my Circus World Museum colleagues, present and past.

Fred Dahlinger, Jr.
Baraboo, Wisconsin
July 21, 2000

The coming of Buffalo Bill's Wild West and Congress of Rough Riders of the World was foretold by colorful and thrilling lithographs that covered hundreds of walls, fences and windows. The men that posted them across the community and throughout the countryside traveled and lived in the advertising car, which moved several weeks in advance of the show. The first advertising car of Buffalo Bill's Wild West was an 1877-built car originally furnished by the Barney & Smith Car Company of Dayton, Ohio, to the Great Forepaugh Show, a large railroad circus. Measuring only about forty feet long, it was typical of the vintage cars that initially carried the wild west in the 1890s. The car was outfitted with an older style link and pin coupler that was phased out by the turn of the century. *Photograph copied by Harry Atwell, 1895, Thomas P. Parkinson Collection, Circus World Museum.*

The advertising car fleet of Buffalo Bill's Wild West was expanded to three vehicles in 1896, including this No. 1 car with vertical board sheathing on the sides. The hoses on the car ends confirm that it was equipped with air brakes. The car is shown here several years later, at the Barnum & Bailey Greatest Show on Earth winter quarters. It was at this site where the show was outfitted for its annual tours from 1895 through 1902, and again when it returned from Europe for the 1907 season. The Buffalo Bill cars were always decorated with finely executed printing. Circuses placed elaborate scenic paintings on the sides of their advertising cars, but the panoramic views illustrating scenes to be observed in the wild west arena were reserved for the show's outstanding lithographs. *Photograph, circa 1899, Bridgeport, Connecticut, Denver Public Library, Western History Collection, NS-236.*

Buffalo Bill's Wild West advertising car No. 2 formerly served the billing crew for W. W. Cole's New Colossal Shows, a medium-sized railroad circus of the 1880s. Small shows fielded one car, but larger operations had as many as three or four cars on the road at the same time, each staffed by up to two-dozen men. When multiple advertising cars were operated, each one of them supported a particular branch of the advance operation, such as billposting, excursion planning or opposition to competing traveling field shows, including circuses. Militaristic words such as "campaign" and "opposition brigade" were used to characterize the confrontational nature of the competition. The tearing down of competing shows paper, and fist fights between opposing show advance crews, were part of the business routine. *Cabinet photograph by Cramer, 1896, Scranton, Pennsylvania, Fred D. Pfening, Jr. Collection.*

At the turn of the century there were about fifteen stock cars in Buffalo Bill's Wild West train. The over 400 draft and saddle horses, elephants, camels, buffalo, burros and oxen that traveled with the wild west were carried in these vehicles. The numerous designs suggest that they came from a variety of show resources under the control of James A. Bailey, who had contractual responsibility for the railroad transport of the show. Their relatively short lengths, less than the contemporary show standard of 60 feet, may indicate that they came from the defunct Adam Forepaugh circus. They would have been over twenty years old. The entire train totaled about 50 cars at this time. The men atop the cars were part of the show's contingent of "Rough Riders." Native Americans appear to be unloading their own horses from one stock car. The car on the far right had some type of sleeping accommodations for animal keepers. The internationally famous William Frederick "Buffalo Bill" Cody is the man in the left foreground. *Photograph, circa 1900, Denver Public Library, Western History Collection, NS-642.*

When wild west exhibitions adopted flat car-type train operation, they utilized the loading and unloading technology that had been perfected by railroad circuses in the 1870s. The wagons that carried all of the equipment and properties necessary to stage the wild west and associated exhibits were carried in four-wheel wagons that were loaded on flat cars. These 60-foot wooden flats appear to be of the same style that the Barney & Smith Car Company furnished to the Barnum & Bailey Greatest Show on Earth with knuckle couplers. It is likely that Barnum & Bailey cars transported the Cody operation while the circus toured Europe from 1898 through 1902. They reverted back to circus duty when the circus returned and the wild west went to Europe from 1903 through 1906. *Photograph by John C. Hemment, circa 1901, Denver Public Library, Western History Collection, F-8571.*

There were about sixty vehicles to place on the wild west flats, a task that consumed a couple hours. The loading rituals of the field shows never failed to mesmerize and excite the imaginations of little boys and grown men of the era, like the one on the left. Baggage wagon 27 has just been pulled to the top of the flat cars by the white pull-up team that will soon turn around and provide the same service to another wagon. The dapple hook rope team on the far left propelled it to the location that it filled on the train. The wagon was secured there with wedge-shaped wood blocks called "chocks" that were jammed into place between the wheels and the car deck. *Photograph, August 9, 1901, Marshalltown, Iowa, Denver Public Library, Western History Collection, NS-703.*

Multiple-sheet show lithographs featuring Johnny Baker, "The Celebrated Crack Shot," provided an interesting backdrop to this loading scene. A team of horses walking alongside the flat car pulled water wagon number 24 of Buffalo Bill's Wild West up the inclined planes, termed "runs." They provided a navigable surface from the ground to the top, or deck, of the flat cars. The wooden sawhorse-like assemblies supporting the runs were called "jacks" by showmen. Despite the danger that a heavy wagon posed during the loading operation to the men that did the work, these "razorbacks" were casually observing something in the background that caught their attention. *Photograph, August 9, 1901, Marshalltown, Iowa, Howard C. Tibbals Collection.*

At one time, Col. Cody traveled in an elaborate Mann Boudoir Car Company private car that previously conveyed singer Adelina Patti to her engagements. In later years he traveled in other private cars. One source states that he once owned the private car utilized by the great American showman P. T. Barnum. Car number 50 lacked the Victorian era elegance of the earlier Mann car, but probably made up for it with more modern conveniences and better construction that provided a more comfortable ride. The estate of James A. Bailey furnished Buffalo Bill's train in 1907 and the Ringlings, who bought out the Bailey interests in the Greatest Show on Earth and the wild west that year, supplied it in 1908. Thereafter the Ringlings sold their interests in Buffalo Bill's Wild West to Gordon W. Lillie, better known as "Pawnee Bill," who had been Cody's principal competitor for nearly twenty years. *Photograph, circa 1907, Buffalo Bill Museum and Grave, Golden, Colorado.*

This narrow vestibule car was the No. 2 advertising car of the Barnum & Bailey Greatest Show on Earth from as early as 1903 through 1906 inclusive. After a four-year tour of Europe, a new train to transport the wild west in the U.S. was assembled from a variety of resources. This car was transferred at that time to Buffalo Bill's Wild West, probably for the season of 1907. It was later purchased for J. H. Eschman's World's United Railroad Shows, a circus, by 1915. The 29 men posed beside the car represented not only the car staff but other wild west show agents. The flamboyant Major John M. Burke can be seen seated on the right side of the ramp, near the middle of the view. *Photograph, circa 1907, Gift, Walter W. Tyson Collection, Circus World Museum.*

Gordon W. Lillie, better known as Pawnee Bill, toured with Buffalo Bill and others between 1883 and 1887 and eventually launched his own wild west exhibition in the fall of 1887. After a few years of difficulty, Pawnee Bill's Wild West prospered and grew into a fine 20 to 25-car operation. The show had only two advertising cars in 1900 but they were numbered 2 and 4 to project the image of a larger operation. Advance Car No. 2, depicted here, had a simple title scheme augmented by two portraits. The painter erred in spelling out one feature, "Rosevelt's (sic) Rough Riders." The "America's National Entertainment" slogan was employed by both the Lillie and Cody operations. *Photograph from 1900 Pawnee Bill's Wild West Route Book, Circus World Museum.*

One of the Pawnee Bill's Wild West's baggage stock, a fine Percheron horse, walked down the run from a stock car to the ground and to the waiting hand of a driver or helper who assembled a team. Baggage stock wore their collars continuously. The horses were packed solid inside the car, sideways, from one end to the other, so that they would not fall over during abrupt changes in train motion. These cars may have been built by the Middletown Car Works, which supplied a number of stocks to Pawnee Bill's operation in the early 1900s. Until that time, it is believed that Lillie leased his cars from a system railroad. *Print from original negative, August 8, 1905, Washington, Iowa, Circus World Museum.*

Two different styles of flat cars carried the wagons of Pawnee Bill's Wild West. They were of the usual wood construction with metal truss rods under the wood sills that formed the frame. Some cars had a multitude of stakes projecting from the outside sills upward to secure the side-boards, or "gunnels," as showmen called them, corrupting the nautical term "gunwales." It does not appear to have been Lillie's practice to adorn every car with his show title. Wild west flats carried an elaborate range of vehicles that included stagecoaches, cannon, prairie schooners, ammunition wagons and carriages, in addition to the usual baggage and parade wagons. *Photograph by Harry V. Bock, circa 1905, courtesy Allen L. Farnum.*

Pawnee Bill took his show off the road after the 1907 tour and spent the summer of 1908 at the Wonderland amusement park in Revere Beach, Massachusetts. He peddled the show's transportation equipment piecemeal to a variety of buyers. One of the sleepers was sold or traded to the Southern Iron & Equipment Company. This view was taken after it arrived in the SI&E yard in Atlanta, Georgia. The show title was painted out to signify the change in ownership. Some of the names applied to the Pawnee Bill's Wild West sleepers were "Hunter," "Rattler," "Oklahoma," "Hazel," "May Lillie" and "Pawnee." *Photograph, April 27, 1909, Atlanta, Georgia, Ray W. Buhrmaster Collection.*

Col. Frederick T. Cummins organized and managed Indian Congress attractions at several world's fairs, including the 1898 Trans-Mississippi Exposition, the 1901 Pan American Exposition and the 1904 Louisiana Purchase Exposition. Like Cody and Lillie, Cummins decided to take his static attraction on tour by framing it as a railroad show for 1906. One of Cummins' partners was former circus proprietor Walter L. Main of Geneva, Ohio, who previously sold his own show in early 1905. A paper remnant of that circus explains the Main title on the bill in the open door. *Photograph, 1906, Howard C. Tibbals Collection.*

Three Miller brothers went into partnership with circus man Edward Arlington to launch the Miller Bros. and Arlington 101 Ranch Real Wild West in 1907. It was a traveling extension of their gigantic Oklahoma ranch and static exhibitions that they had staged there and elsewhere. Their new and well-financed 25 to 30-car operation provided immediate competition to Buffalo Bill's Wild West. They injected the adjective "real" into the title, casting aspersions on Cody's show and its diverse multi-cultural presentations. The unloading of a great wild west operation attracted the same kind of crowds as a circus train arrival. The stock cars that contained horses were on the left. The nearly solid-sided stock cars further back hauled elephants, camels and other sensitive exotic beasts. The flat cars on the right were loaded with the show's baggage and parade wagons, and other performance vehicles, there being no wild animal cages on this, or any other, bonafide wild west operation. *Photograph, circa 1910, Howard C. Tibbals Collection.*

The sleepers and private cars of the 101 Ranch show bore the names of some of the show's principals. "Mister Eddie" was obviously Edward Arlington and Joe Miller was one of the three Millers, the other two being Zach and George C. The narrow vestibule car in the bottom view was similar to others that were with Arlington's independent 1913 show, the Arlington & Beckman Wild West. The open platform car had ironwork that can be found on several vintage cars that were with other traveling shows. Passenger cars were the most expensive vehicles in any show train and represented a significant capital investment. *Photograph, circa 1910, Howard C. Tibbals Collection.*

This 101 Ranch billposting crew had an early automobile to aid in their distribution of show publicity materials. It loaded into the advertising car via a pair of runs that were placed at the end of the car. The large doors that folded back to accommodate the vehicle can be seen on the right. Later 101 Ranch crews used additional autos and also Indian-make motorcycles to propel them to their duties with great speed. The Millers outfit last toured under their leadership in 1916, with others owning the property in 1917. *Photograph by Swearingen, 1912, Guthrie, Oklahoma, Gift, Walter W. Tyson, Circus World Museum.*

Kit Carson's Buffalo Ranch Wild West was the 1911-1914 operation of a showman named Thomas F. Wiedemann. Some of his railroad equipment and wagons came from William P. Hall, a Lancaster, Missouri, broker of show chattel, but most of it had been the Jones Bros. Buffalo Ranch Wild West the previous year. Wiedemann's train included five sleepers in 1913. One of them, on the far right, was a very unusual vehicle that may have been converted from another type of railroad car. Similar enclosed sleepers were with the Orton, Great Wallace and John Robinson circuses, where they housed workingmen in high-density bunks. Wiedemann's show was in the fifteen to twenty-car class, making it smaller than the Two Bills and 101 Ranch troupes. *Photograph, 1913, Howard C. Tibbals Collection.*

The Barnum & Bailey Greatest Show on Earth had several identical advertising cars from as early as 1896 to as late as 1904. One or two of them, including the car illustrated here, were transferred to Buffalo Bill's Wild West operation in 1907 or 1908 and at least one remained there through 1913. The railroad equipment became the property of Pawnee Bill via a purchase that he made from the Ringling brothers in 1908. In 1909 the show rolled out as Buffalo Bill's Wild West Combined With Pawnee Bill's Great Far East. Sometimes the names of the two principals were transposed, as on their No. 2 advertising car. The "possum" belly under the car housed brushes, buckets and other materials needed by the billposters that erected the fantastic lithographs printed for the wild west. Their ladders were secured to the roof of the car. *Photograph, circa 1910, Howard C. Tibbals Collection.*

The combined Lillie and Cody show was the largest wild west effort, in terms of the number of railroad cars, ever organized. At one time the show moved on sixty cars. To either expand or upgrade the rail car complement of the combined "Two Bills" show, as it was known in the business, an order was placed with the Standard Steel Car Company of Pittsburgh, Pennsylvania, for sixty-foot long steel-frame stock and flat cars for the season of 1911. They were the first conventional steel cars made for any traveling show and represented both a significant investment and a departure from the wood cars that had hauled shows for forty years. The stocks were rated at 80,000 pounds capacity. Though the frames and superstructure were all steel, wood planking was still utilized to enclose the car sides and to form the roof. This car had a heavy fabricated center sill arrangement that eliminated the need for additional trussing. Several of the Standard Steel stocks later served with circuses and railroad carnivals. *Photograph, 1911, Butler, Pennsylvania, courtesy Standard Steel Car Company, and Keith Retterer.*

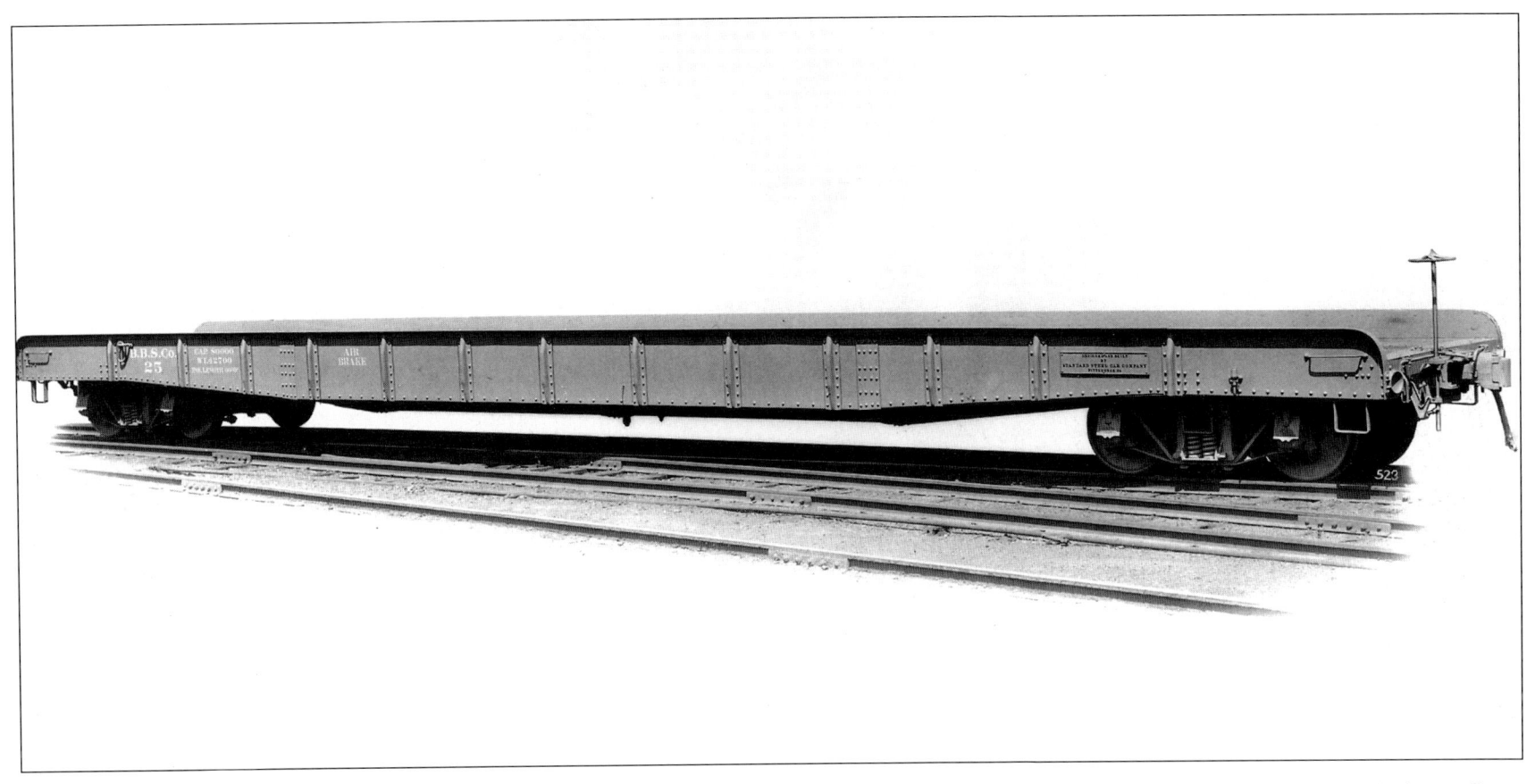

The Two Bills steel flat cars had a very distinctive side profile that distinguished them from other steel show flats that had a "fish belly" design. The descriptive term arose from the drop in the center of the car that reminded one viewer of the lower contour of a fish. Made entirely of steel except for the wood decking, they were rated at 80,000 pounds carrying capacity. The heavy steel draft sills and side fabrications eliminated the need for trussing under the frames. Note the cast builder's plate on the right and the "B. B. S. Co." inscription on the left, presumably an abbreviation for Buffalo Bill Show Company. The brake wheel and shaft on the end of the car pivoted downward and away from the coupler, providing clearance for the passage of wagons from car to car. These cars became the property of a circus man, J.A. Jones, in the 1910s, and were then dispersed in the 1920s to several circuses and carnivals. *Photograph, 1911, Butler, Pennsylvania, courtesy Standard Steel Car Company, and Keith Retterer.*

Another of the medium-sized wild west troupes that flourished in the early 1910s was Young Buffalo's Wild West. Young Buffalo was a fictitious persona who resembled Buffalo Bill, particularly in terms of his facial hair and clothing. The troupe was actually owned by a showman named Vernon C. Seaver. It was among the larger wild west troupes, being in the twenty to twenty-five car size. This sleeper probably served as the rolling home for the car's namesake and show owner, along with other staff members. The Col. Cummins Far East name was appended to the title by 1912. The show last toured in 1914. *Photograph, circa 1911, Howard C. Tibbals Collection.*

The only known interior view of a wild west advertising car is this dimly-lit shot of the Young Buffalo's Wild West vehicle. The layout would have been similar to circus advertising cars of the same era. In the immediate foreground were the wide side doors that could be opened for the movement of large bundles of lithographs and buckets of paste. Beyond them were counters for the assembling of groups of specific lithographs for the various billposters. At the far end were the crew living quarters, including a small office for the car manager. *Photograph, 1911, courtesy The Billboard.*

The three Miller brothers decided to go back into show business in the 1920s and purchased Andrew Downie's circus as the physical basis for their new wild west operation. This advertising car had previously supported the advance efforts for Downie's show and then extolled the merits of the Miller Bros. 101 Ranch Real Wild West. Note that the car was outfitted with end loading doors that enabled the carrying of a vehicle for route work. The date sheet was one of hundreds that the billposters erected in the community. Clyde Willard, the Car Manager, was in the back row, sixth from the left. One can only imagine the dramatic color scheme that enlivened the exterior of this car. *Photograph by Glen S. Cook, 1925, Albany, New York, Howard C. Tibbals Collection.*

One of the Miller brothers, probably Zach, just gave the command "trunk" to one of their Asiatic elephants. She responded accordingly by raising her head and curling her trunk upwards in a characteristic pose. The Miller brothers, who prided themselves on the authenticity of their wild west demonstrations, found it necessary to include circus-type activity in their arena presentations in order to hold the attention of their flapper-era audiences. The wood frame elephant car shown here, with small ventilator openings, was undoubtedly part of the train acquired from Andrew Downie. *Print from original negative by Harry A. Atwell, 1926, Circus World Museum.*

The Mt. Vernon Car Manufacturing Company of Mt. Vernon, Illinois, fabricated steel frame stock cars for the Miller brothers use in February 1925. They were rated at 60,000 pounds capacity and measured 70 feet long inside. These cars were similar to others made by Mt. Vernon for various circuses as early as 1920. Mt. Vernon stocks can be identified by the absence of a diagonal brace in the two end panels of the truss that framed the car sides. Some stock car doors were hinged, like these, while others rolled or slid to the side. *Photograph, 1925, Mt. Vernon, Illinois, Howard C. Tibbals Collection.*

There were at least five new steel frame Mt. Vernon-built stocks with the 101 Ranch in its first season. A number of older wood stocks, like the one on the far left, continued to serve the show through 1931. Some of the fine quality baggage stock used by the Miller operation can be seen in this view. Following unloading from the cars, the horses were made up into the teams that pulled the wagons from the rail yard to the show grounds. Also note the one mule, part of the team that pulled a prairie schooner in the Miller street parade and performance arena. With all of the animal and human activity in the midst of a busy railroad operation, it is understandable why there were often mishaps involving show people and beasts in the yards. *Photograph by Harry A. Atwell, 1926, Gift, Harry A. Atwell, Circus World Museum.*

The Miller outfit was the only large wild west aggregation operating during the mid-1920s. Most of the Miller wagons continued to load onto the wood flats that came with the Downie show purchase. These appear to be the slightly longer than 60-foot cars that Downie bought for his Walter L. Main America's Best Shows in 1921 and 1922. They were among the first show cars made by the Haffner-Thrall Car Company of Chicago, Illinois. Cars of this type could also be found in several carnival trains of the 1920s and 1930s. The slight sag in the middle of these cars indicates that they had been used for some time carrying heavy loads. *Photograph, circa 1926, Circus World Museum.*

The Mt. Vernon Car Manufacturing Company furnished a number of 70-foot long, 60,000-pounds capacity steel flats of their fish belly design. The simple title scheme on the cars can be seen only in builder photographs. The show may have immediately painted over the builder's paint in a more flamboyant manner after the cars arrived at the wild west's Oklahoma winter quarters. Despite the purchase of several new steel flats, the Millers continued to own wood frame flat cars through the final season of 1931. *Photograph, 1925, Mt. Vernon, Illinois, Howard C. Tibbals Collection.*

In some years the Ranch show sleeping cars were decorated with large block lettering that was readable from a considerable distance. This car probably had all arch windows at one time but was modified through the years to a hybrid appearance. Steel plates have been applied over the original wood sheathing. It was not unusual for former railroad and Pullman cars to serve twenty years in their original capacity, and to then serve several more decades in show service. *Photograph, circa 1927, Howard C. Tibbals Collection.*

This classy looking arch window observation car served to house one or more of the Miller brothers when they traveled with the 30-car show that bore their family and ranch name. The stained glass design and other features confirm that the Hicks Locomotive and Car Works of Chicago Heights, Illinois, made the car. Hicks constructed three such cars in 1909. The observation was a wood car and had no major structural steel elements in the frame. Though the car was nearly two decades old by the time this photograph was taken, it had not lost any of its sparkle and shine. Note that the stained glass panels are still intact in all locations. *Photograph, circa 1925, courtesy The Glass Negative, Ray and Velma Falconer.*

The Warren Tank Car Company of Warren, Pennsylvania, furnished three stock cars and six flat cars to the Buck Jones Wild West Shows and Round-Up Days for a tour in 1929. They were 72-feet long and rated at either 40 or 50-ton capacity. Similar cars were furnished to many carnivals and a few circuses in the 1920s. Flat car number 15 was termed a "run car" because it had special attachments necessary for the loading and unloading of wagons. The runs can be seen at the far left. Two pair of brackets were in the center of the car for holding the "snubber" posts, devices used in the unloading of the flats. *Photograph, 1929, Joseph S. Rettinger Collection.*

Not even the personal appearances by Buck Jones could keep the wild west that carried his name solvent. It failed in mid-July 1929, having been on tour for only two months. After closing, the Warren-built cars were returned to the manufacturer but the five Jones sleepers were sent to the William P. Hall farm where they eventually disappeared. This arch window vehicle was named "Eagle," after one of Jones's horses, while a companion car carried the name "Maxine" in honor of Jones's daughter. *Photograph by Ralph Miller, circa 1934, Lancaster, Missouri, Circus World Museum.*

Ken Maynard was another movie matinee idol that decided he wanted a wild west aggregation. Railroad circus owner George Christy of South Houston, Texas, sold him a number of parade, cage and baggage wagons that comprised his former Lee Bros. circus. Flat cars to haul the wagons were hired from the Atchison, Topeka & Santa Fe Railroad. The cars were used only once, to ferry equipment from Christy's winter quarters to Maynard's location in southern California. Maynard's show never made it off his ranch, where just a few public performances were given. Several enclosed cars were part of the train that conveyed Maynard's Texas purchases to California. The cars may have been intended to haul stock, but their sides were solid and they provided no ventilation. They had side trusses characteristic of Warren manufacture, but their origin and prior usage is unknown. It was highly unusual to have the show title extend across two cars as illustrated in this view. *Photograph by Bert Chipman, 1936, San Diego, California, Joseph S. Rettinger Collection.*

One of the finest shows to ever take to the rails was Col. Tim McCoy's Real Wild West of 1938. With the exception of the advance and sleeping cars, it was built entirely new from the ground up. Unfortunately, it made its debut in one of the worst years of the Depression, 1938, and never really had a chance to survive. The dapper advance crew of the show was photographed beside their advertising car before the season commenced. They anticipated a bright future for their marvelous new show, but the chill in the air had them bundled up against the cold spring winds. *Photograph by Harry A. Atwell, 1938, Gift, Harry A. Atwell, Circus World Museum.*

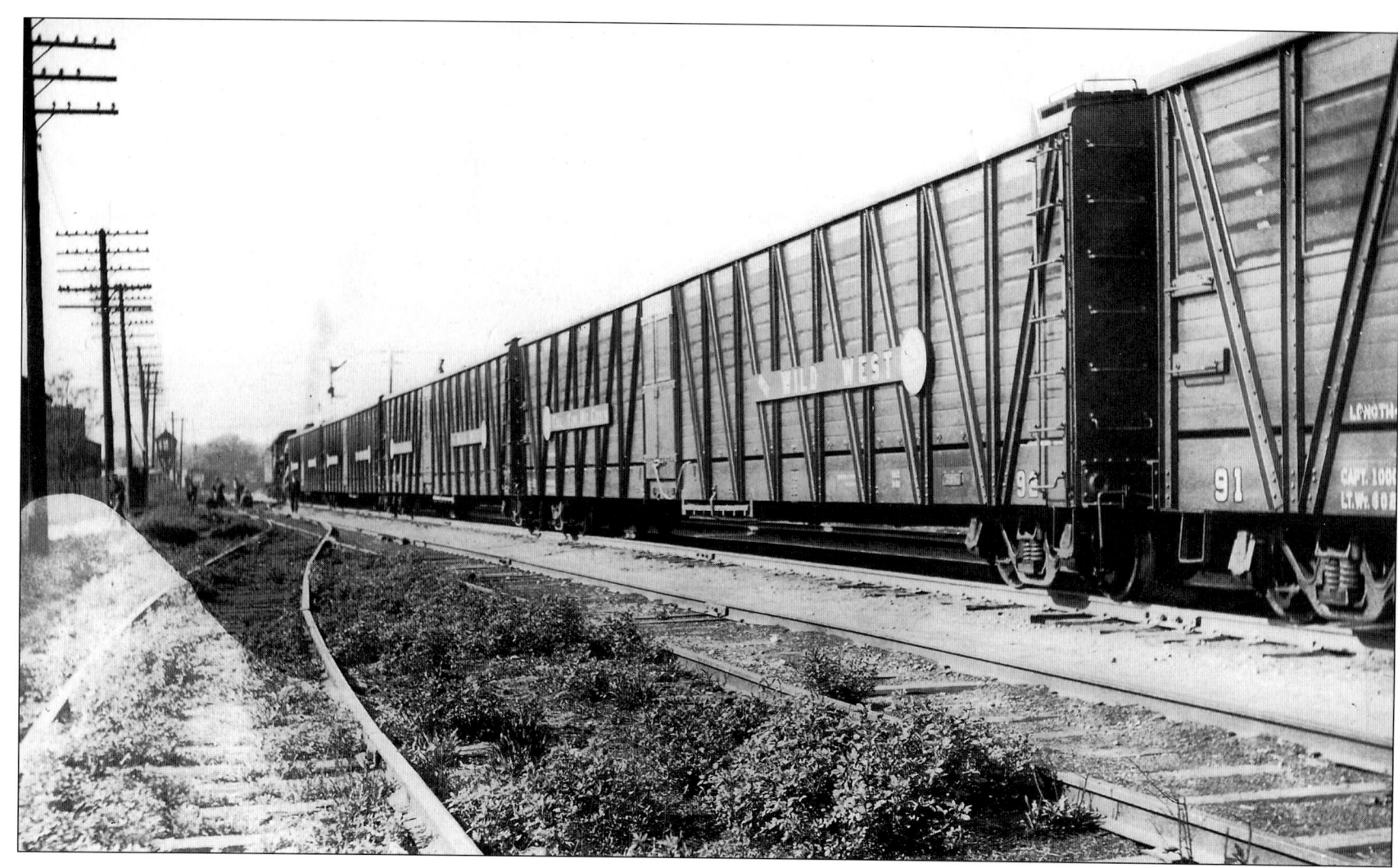

The Warren Tank Car Company fabricated all of the new stock and flat cars for the McCoy show. There were eight stocks, each 72 feet long and rated at 100,000 pounds carrying capacity. They all appear to have been identical in design and construction. There was little interest in the stock cars after the show closed because there were fewer shows hauling a lesser number of horses. The McCoy stocks were abandoned, scrapped or altered into flat cars. Two were acquired by the World of Mirth Shows by the early 1940s. Another one or two languished as a storage facility in a Washington, D.C. area railroad yard until the mid-1970s. *Photograph, April 26, 1938, Dayton, Ohio, Circus World Museum.*

The twelve flat cars furnished by the Warren Tank Car Company were of the same design that had been furnished to other shows. They were 72 feet long and had a capacity of 100,000 pounds. Just to the left of the handbrake was a cast plate that read "Warren Tank Car Co./Warren, Penna./Owner and Lessor." The McCoy show did not have clear title to the cars, being financed by the car fabricator. The two McCoy run cars were later sold at auction to the Johnny J. Jones Exposition and the remaining ten flats went to the Hennies Bros. Shows, another major railroad carnival. The successor to Warren Tank Car Company, Warren Railcar Service, Inc., undertakes railroad car maintenance today. *Photograph by Harry A. Atwell, 1938, Gift, Harry A. Atwell Collection, Circus World Museum.*

The rituals of show unloading still attracted a crowd despite the lean economic times of 1938. Little did anyone know that they were witnessing the last wild west operation to travel by rails. One of the McCoy stock cars had already disgorged its horses and men were placing the run underneath the car frame. The next car was being unloaded and soon the baggage stock would be attached to the wagons that were unloaded from the flat cars in the background. It was the last great demonstration of equine horsepower by a traveling show. *Photograph, April 26, 1938, Dayton, Ohio, Circus World Museum.*

The Springfield Wagon and Trailer Company of Springfield, Missouri, supplied an entirely new fleet of steel-bodied wagons with dual pneumatic tires for McCoy's new wild west railer. With the wagons gleaming in white and the flats painted a brilliant blue, the loaded train was a beautiful sight. It was the most modern traveling show of its time, with a quality fleet of transportation vehicles that could not be matched by any other traveling show. The adjacent Mack Bulldog truck and stagecoach provided an interesting visual counterpoint of technology. *Photograph by Harry Atwell, 1938, Springfield, Illinois, Circus World Museum.*

The run on the right was set, but the men struggled to move the heavy steel run on the left into its proper location. Some men placed the support jacks into position while others gathered the board shims that would be used to make the support solid from the run to the ground. Many of the men observing the action would have been willing to take a job with the McCoy outfit, no matter how hard the work. The show provided three square meals a day and a bed to sleep in at night. *Photograph, April 26, 1938, Dayton, Ohio, Circus World Museum.*

Wagons number 52 and 51, hauling the McCoy blacksmith shop and stable, respectively, were the fifth and sixth wagons of the day to be unloaded. The pull-over team that delivered wagon 51 to the runs has already started its return to pick up the next wagon. The poler who steered the wagon to the end of the flats leaped across the runs, apparently knowing that he would have enough time to get across before the wagon made its descent to the ground. *Photograph, April 26, 1938, Dayton, Ohio, Circus World Museum.*

The only non-white wagon on the McCoy show was the light blue ticket wagon. The poler has nearly completed his assignment of guiding the wagon to the runs and is about to move out of the way. The man at the rear has attached the "hook rope." The body of the rope has been wound around a "snubber post" in the middle of the flat. The friction between the rope and the post was used to reduce the speed of the wagon as it rolled down the runs to the ground. *Photograph, April 26, 1938, Dayton, Ohio, Circus World Museum.*

Five of the McCoy show sleepers were refitted parlor cars acquired from the Pullman Company in February and March 1938. These cars were originally built between 1901 and 1904 and adapted to other purposes in the 1920s. Like the remainder of the McCoy train, the sleepers were all painted in a very tasteful manner that featured the show title and the show's insignia. Col. Tim McCoy traveled in a bit more luxury in his own private car, the open platform observation car "Cheyenne." *Photograph, April 26, 1938, Dayton, Ohio, Circus World Museum.*

Professor Gentry was actually Henry B. Gentry of Bloomington, Indiana. At one time, he and his brothers had four independent dog and pony troupes on tour across the United States. Their diminutive animals, including dogs, ponies, monkeys and small elephants, made them a favorite with children and their mothers. Initially the Gentry productions appeared on opera house stages, in horticultural halls and at other indoor venues, but later they carried their own tent for outdoor appearances. The Ohio Falls Car Company furnished or repaired car number 1 in the 1890s. The baggage door and barred ventilator openings suggest that it hauled baggage, animals, and their keepers. *Photograph, undated, Jeffersonville, Indiana, courtesy ACF Industries and Frank M. Ellington.*

Another Gentry car associated with the Ohio Falls Car Company was their number 2. It possibly provided the living accommodations for the owner, and the staff and working people of the show, complementing car number 1. It was still common to apply fine painted detail and pinstriping on cars at the time. Note the takeoff of the familiar registered Ringling Bros. and Barnum & Bailey Combined Shows trademark, "The Greatest Show on Earth for Ladies and Children." The Gentry operation eventually grew into two large flat car-type operations that were essentially complete circuses, but on a physical scale for youngsters. *Card photograph, undated, Jeffersonville, Indiana, Howard C. Tibbals Collection.*

This three-car Gentry Bros. train included some very unusual vehicles. The two cars on the left appear to have been arranged for the transportation and care of stock, such as the dogs and ponies featured by the troupe. The car on the far left was also outfitted with end loading doors to accommodate the loading of vehicles. The purpose of the poles on the roof of the middle car has not been determined. *Photograph, circa 1899, Gift, Harry L. Kelly Collection, Tom Kelly, Circus World Museum.*

Sipe & Dolman's America's Greatest Dog & Pony Shows was another of the more than dozen educated dog and pony outfits that originated in the last quarter of the nineteenth century. It was organized in Kokomo, Indiana, in 1895. This Ohio Falls Car Company vehicle bore the number three, suggesting that there were two other cars in the operation. Note that the identical "Dogs and Ponies that Almost Talk" legend could also be found on the No. 2 Gentry car. Like the Gentry operation, the Sipe show evolved into a complete flat car type show shortly after the turn of the century. The last of these dog and pony show operations survived until 1922. Only their name survives today, meaning the demonstrations that staff or sales people stage in a demonstrative way for management or prospective clients. *Photograph, circa 1896, Jeffersonville, Indiana, courtesy ACF Industries and Frank M. Ellington.*

The exciting actions taken to extinguish fires and rescue threatened building occupants made the demonstration of fire fighting techniques a popular attraction at the turn of the century. Fire fighting shows were staged on world's fair midways and in amusement parks and resorts across America. Chief George C. Hale of the Kansas City Fire Department organized the most famous of the fire shows. Though it traveled on a train of 22 cars in 1906, no photographs of it are known to exist. Another "flames" outfit, Talbot's Fighting the Flames, was captured on film. This was the show's advertising car. *Photograph, 1906, Circus World Museum.*

Circus men C. Lee Williams, John O. Talbot and Frank Tate joined together to organize the Talbot's Fighting the Flames Spectacle for the season of 1906. Organized like any other form of outdoor show, it had three stock cars for the horses that pulled the show's wagons, fifteen flats for the wagons and four sleepers for the owners, staff and working people. It moved each and every day to a new community, staged a daily street parade, burned down the same portable buildings and saved the same threatened people at each and every engagement under a canvas tent. The sleeping car "Tate" was obviously named for one of the show owners. *Photograph, 1906, Fred D. Pfening, Jr. Collection.*

Several stock and flat combination cars were made for circuses and other traveling shows. The stock portion probably housed horses while the flat car area was a place to carry wagons or carriages. Edna Marretta was a principal bareback rider with circuses between 1900 and 1909 and may have used this car for other riding ventures. This wood frame car measured 65 feet long. *Photograph, 1900, Jeffersonville, Indiana, John W. Barriger III National Railroad Library, St. Louis Mercantile Library, University of Missouri-St. Louis.*

A Zamboni, the self-propelled machine that smooths the ice for skaters by scraping off the surface and then depositing a fresh layer of water to freeze, leads a group of baggage wagons out of the tunnel cars that transported the equipment of Morris Chalfen's three-car Holiday on Ice troupe. The ice shows relied upon the technology devised for the 1960 Ringling Bros. and Barnum & Bailey Combined Shows operations to design their train cars. These three dark orange vehicles were former Pennsylvania Railroad cars. *Photograph, circa 1963, Atlanta, Georgia, Thomas P. Parkinson Collection, Circus World Museum.*

The Kickapoo Indian Medicine Company operated a fleet of advertising cars that heralded the arrival of their shows. This was car number 17. The Kickapoo Indian Medicine Company promoted the sale of their Kickapoo Indian Sagwa, essentially a patent medicine that can generously be termed a cure for just about anything that ailed a human being. They visited communities for days on end to promote the product with various types of demonstrations. The crews that traveled in the advance cars advertised the impending arrival of the encampments, complete with teepees, a stage, and other show apparatus necessary to sell the "medicine." *Photograph, circa 1910, Fred D. Pfening, Jr. Collection.*

Alexander Herrmann, billed as Herrmann the Great, was one of the greatest magicians of all time. Everything about Herrmann, his stage presence, his horses and carriage, and his own train, established him as the quintessential showman. Appropriate to his stature in the business and a rather imperial manner, he traveled across America in a special three-car train that could be coupled to regularly scheduled passenger trains. One of the vehicles was a baggage car to haul show props and the other was a palatial private car. It is thought that this car carried the horses and carriage of which Herrmann was so fond and proud. *Photograph, circa 1892, Jeffersonville, Indiana, courtesy George Anderson.*

This is a different car than number 3, a conclusion reached by noting the presence of the clerestory. Magic or illusion props and stage equipment can be very heavy apparatus and are usually housed in heavy wooden crates specially designed for their cargo's needs. The interior of Herrmann the Great's baggage car was outfitted with sacrificial floor and wall panels to take the abuse from the handling of these heavy and awkward loads. The car had at least four pair of sliding doors to facilitate handling of the baggage. *Photograph, circa 1892, Jeffersonville, Indiana, courtesy George Anderson.*

The third car in Herrmann's train was a fine private car with elegant Victorian era decorations. Reportedly the car had once been the "Lalee," the rolling home of Lily Langtry. Following Herrmann's death on the car on December 17, 1896, it was allegedly sold to Flo Ziegfeld, who provided it for the use of his star Anna Held. Under the name "Olympia" or "Olympic" it served a few more years before being retired to the Philadelphia train yards for special events. *Photograph, circa 1895, courtesy David Meyer, Magic Collectors Association LLC.*

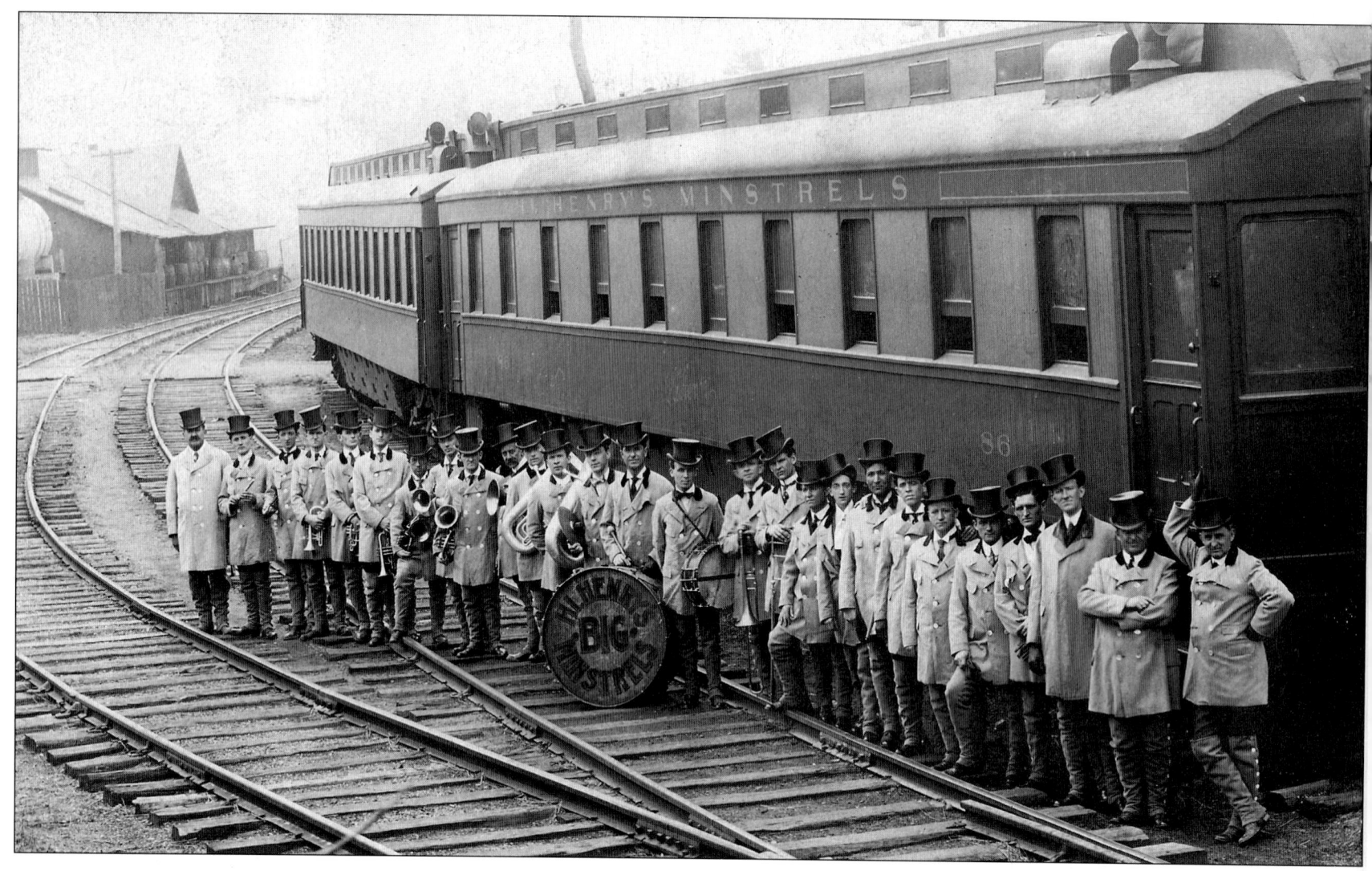

Minstrel shows are generally remembered as being indoor operations, on theater stages. After the turn of the century, several minstrel shows toured by railroad car and played under canvas tents. A number of enterprising showmen made a fortune with that type of operation. Col. Hiram Patrick "Hi" Henry was an early operator of traveling minstrel shows. He organized Hi Henry's Minstrels in 1879 and until nearly the end of the enterprise he usually presented a short specialty on the cornet to his audiences. The Hi Henry Minstrels was a two-car operation as early as 1889, but this view dates to after the turn of the century. *Postcard photograph, circa 1907, Circus World Museum.*

Roy E. Fox was known for his Roy E. Fox's Popular Players, a repertoire tent theater troupe that toured by rail car from the early 1900s into the mid-1910s. The band from another of his undertakings, Roy E. Fox's Lone Star Minstrels, posed in front of their highly decorated sleeper, the "Irene." *Card photograph, circa 1910, Circus World Museum.*

Harvey's Greater Minstrels toured on this two-car setup in the early 1920s. The owner, R. M. Harvey, was best known for his many years of service as a circus agent. At one time he was a partner in a minstrel show with P. G. Lowery, a great African-American circus cornettist. The show featured 45 people, including a concert band, an octoroon beauty chorus and twelve high class vaudeville acts, and considered itself a "big city show" according to self-proclaimed statements on the show letterhead. Harvey is on the far right. *Photograph, circa 1922, Gift, R. M. Harvey Collection, Circus World Museum.*

William Cameron Coup will always be remembered for successfully converting the P. T. Barnum's Great Traveling World's Fair into the world's first large and complete railroad tent circus in 1872. His career path plunged thereafter, with the demise of his W. C. Coup's New United Monster Shows in 1882 and several small dog and pony show operations in the late 1880s. For 1891 he launched his Enchanted Rolling Palaces enterprise that attempted to capitalize on the great appeal of the dime museum. Coup essentially mounted a museum on rails, within the confines of seven or eight railroad cars, and routed it across America. The car on the left was probably one of the two Arms Palace Horse Car Company vehicles with Coup's two-car 1889 Equescurriculum. The St. Charles Car Company manufactured five additional, elaborately decorated, white and gold museum train cars. Despite Coup's articulate manner and visionary nature, this combination Eden Musee, aquarium and auditorium on wheels never clicked with the general public. *Photograph from Chester Photo Service, 1891, Circus World Museum.*

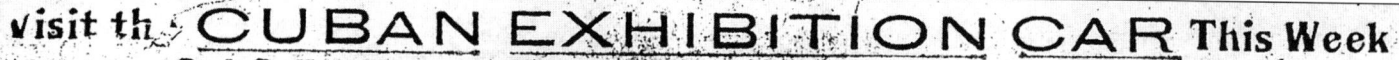

Visit the CUBAN EXHIBITION CAR This Week

On I. C. Tracks, Wood Street Crossing, Monday to Saturday, June 5 to 10.

CITY OF HAVANA. CUBA ON WHEELS. EXPOSITION CAR

Representing the Bureau of Immigration and Department of Agriculture of Cuba. Enroute to Portland Fair. "It is a splendid representation of Cuba. You can spend a whole day in the car and then not see all there is in it."—Atlanta, Ga., Journal. "One of the chief attractions of our Spring Festival was the Cuba on Wheels Car."—Chattanooga News. "Cuba on Wheels is attracting great attention and and the car is being visited daily by a large number of people. Tourists who have seen it are talking of extending their trip to Cuba."—Florida Times, Jacksonville. "The displays are not only instructive but highly entertaining."—Nashville Banner. "It is a choice bit of foreign land in which Americans should be interested."—The State, Columbia, S. C. "It is equal to a trip to the island."—Peoria, Ill., Star. "Distinctly an educational exhibit."—Chicago Journal. "The resources of Cuba are clearly shown."—St. Louis Star. "An Exposition in itself."—Kansas City World. "An exhibit Hot Springs considers herself fortunate in obtaining."—Sentinel Record. "Of special interest are the relics of "THE MAINE"—(property of the United States Government).

OPEN 9 A. M. TO 10 P. M.   **ADMISSION 10 CENTS**

The Spanish-American War raised the interest of Americans in the small island less than 100 miles off the coast of Florida. To satisfy the American curiosity, an enterprising individual conceived of the idea to mount a rail car exhibition of various aspects of Cuban culture and heritage. It was one of many such cars and entire trains that promoted the interests of railroads, states, history, culture, products and communities throughout the 20th century. *Clipping from unidentified newspaper, 1905, Circus World Museum.*

The closing of the western frontier brought with it a great desire among Americans to learn about that which it had just lost. Cody conceived of his wild west to fill the gap, first on stage and then as a traveling show. In a similar way, theatrical producers Peck & Fursman created a show titled "On The Trail, or Daniel Boone the Pioneer" by early 1888. Either a licensee of the firm or an imitator was the one-car troupe called "The New 'On the Trail' or Daniel Boone and Specialty Company." Affiliated with the operation were the Busby brothers of Pana, Illinois. A knock down wagon that hauled the show apparatus fitted in the possum belly under the car frame. Beyond a Daniel Boone character, the outfit also had Native Americans, Cossacks, a brass band, a cage of deer pulled by horses and a bear. *Photograph, 1891, Hastings, Nebraska, Robert S. MacDougall Collection.*

J. M. Busby of Pana, Illinois, operated many different traveling theater organizations under several different names during his career. His Cook Bros. baggage car number 999 carried baggage and people for his temperance production "Ten Nights in a Bar Room." This is the 76-foot long car that was announced as being built for the show in 1901. Note that it had doors at the far end for the loading of vehicles and perhaps horses. At one time a steam calliope was mounted on the roof of the car to announce the show's arrival. This combine, which hauled people and baggage, was fabricated at the Terre Haute, Indiana, shop of the American Car & Foundry Company. *Photograph, 1901, John W. Barriger III National Railroad Library, St. Louis Mercantile Library, University of Missouri-St. Louis.*

Charles H. Yale's "The Way of the Transgressor" sounds as though it was a moralistic play that was enlivened with the addition of a troupe of trained dogs. Some traveling shows employed various forms of stage technology to recreate outdoor activities on a theater stage. For example, a treadmill was used in one production of Lew Wallace's novel *Ben Hur* to re-create the exciting chariot race. Perhaps the Yale production included a moving backdrop, or panorama, to simulate travel on a grand scale in the minds of the viewers. This baggage car could have hauled stage apparatus. The lack of ventilation suggests that it did not carry the Landseer dogs. Yale was a known production manager in his own time, having worked for Gus Hill and other notable theater owners. *Print from original negative, 1905, Wilmington, Delaware, Jackson & Sharp Collection, Delaware Public Archives.*

About 1904 Charles Geyer launched a railroad-based canvas theater troupe. It was on two cars by 1906. His canvas tent and all appurtenances were destroyed in a fire at Roscoe, Texas, on April 27, 1907. He recovered quickly, because by early 1908 he had possession of this fine looking open platform observation car that was serviced by the St. Charles, Missouri, plant of the American Car and Foundry Company. *Photograph, circa 1908, John W. Barriger III National Railroad Library, St. Louis Mercantile Library, University of Missouri-St. Louis.*

Hailing from Urbana, Ohio, when Billy Single Clifford (actually William Clifford Shyrigh) was ten years old he became a circus drummer and then a proficient tap dancer. He appeared in musical comedy and in vaudeville. He and Maud Huth, his one-time wife, played the big theater circuit and also traveled abroad. During his domestic travels he was comfortably ensconced in his private car "Middy." His new show, "Believe Me," opened at Urbana before a hometown audience, and then moved on this car for the first time to Chicago. *Postcard photograph, July 21, 1913, Urbana, Ohio, Howard C. Tibbals Collection.*

Circus musicians Al Kadell and J. S. Kritchfield partnered about 1906 to take out a one-car tent show featuring the enduringly popular "Ten Nights in a Bar Room" and "Uncle Tom's Cabin." The partnership endured until about 1920, when they split. Thereafter Kritchfield fielded a dramatic company that played dates under a canvas tent. Both men eventually returned to the circus business. In a 1916 letter, Kritchfield stated that their 80-foot car cost them $1500. From left to right it contained an office (the first three windows, with two berths), Kritchfield's stateroom (double window), another stateroom (two small windows), another stateroom (double window), another office, then six more staterooms, the kitchen, dining room and 22 feet of baggage space. More storage space was available in the possum belly. *Photograph, circa 1916, Circus World Museum.*

Leo Blondin (inset, real name Baldwin) operated a variety of traveling shows, including theater, moving picture and Uncle Tom's Cabin troupes. In his later years he was known as an elephant handler and worked at the Lincoln Park Zoo in Oklahoma City. While his baggage car and an observation car also in his possession in 1916 were quite conventional, the bottom car was truly unique. Built between 1884 and 1890 according to the cylindrical metal car concept advanced by Edward Y. Robbins, any number of fables accompanied it. It had the sort of look and unusual appearance that would have appealed to a show impresario. Another outdoor showman, W. A. Eiler, definitely owned it in 1907. "Cowboy, Indian and the Lady" was probably one of The Blondin Show's stage productions. Another favorite was his presentation of "Jesse James." *Photograph, undated, Joseph S. Rettinger Collection.*

Leon W. Washburn achieved great success with his Stetson's Uncle Tom's Cabin Company operation. It was presumably named in honor of John Stetson Jr., an important theater magnate of the time. Washburn also operated a circus in the 1890s and early 1900s and then a railroad carnival in the 1910s. It was said that he lost money with all of his shows and would take out an Uncle Tom's Cabin outfit to secure his next bankroll. This special combination car was fabricated to haul either carved pony floats or a steam calliope wagon, horses and other baggage of the show. Tom shows frequently staged a street demonstration to attract attention to their engagements and in the case of Washburn, he had an entire fleet of wagons made especially for the purpose. *Photograph, circa 1896, J. G. Brill Co. Collection, Mss 1556, #425, The Historical Society of Pennsylvania.*

For decades, many showmen made a good living by bringing Harriet Beecher Stowe's *Uncle Tom's Cabin* to life on the stage or in a tent. Those that were traveling tent shows operated like a circus, with trains, wagons, horses, marching bands and daily street parades. Some included special carved floats presenting scenes from the play, or even a steam calliope. One of the finest of the "Tom" show trains was the three-car assembly that carried Al W. Martin's Uncle Tom's Cabin Company. Car number 3 is shown at the Jackson & Sharp Company railroad car plant where it may have been re-decorated or repaired for another long tour on the rails. It hauled the show baggage. Car number 1 was a sleeper for performers and perhaps working people on the show. Martin's private car, "Kitty," was car number 2. *Photograph, circa 1898, Wilmington, Delaware, Circus World Museum.*

Captured and embalmed whales were housed in railroad cars and exhibited in the interior of the United States as early as 1881. The most successful such business was the Pacific Whaling Company, an operation put together by M. C. Hutton and Harold L. Anfenger, a wax museum operator. Between 1928 and 1940 their firm toured a number of whale shows around the United States in special railroad cars. Transporting the dead beasts around the country was a simple problem as compared to keeping them in a condition that did not turn visitors' stomachs from the smell of decay or formaldehyde. *Photograph by Harry A. Atwell, circa 1930, Chicago, Illinois, Thomas P. Parkinson Collection, Circus World Museum.*

Special track was laid to an open block in crowded metropolitan Chicago for the movement of the enclosed car that hauled an embalmed finback whale. After placement, the car sides were opened to form part of the exhibition facility. Additional platforms, railings and awnings augmented the rail car fittings. Once open, the show did a "whale" of a business, everyone and his brother coming to see the mountainous mass of blubber. Reportedly a quarter of a million people passed through this exhibit during a six-week stay. After serving as whale hearses for up to a decade or more, a number of the special cars were converted to circus and carnival stock, box and flat cars, continuing in show service into the 1950s. *Photographs by Harry A. Atwell, circa 1930, Chicago, Illinois, Thomas P. Parkinson Collection, Circus World Museum.*

Most repertoire theater troupes traveled overland by truck and automobile. They would stay a week in most communities, offering a different stage presentation each night. The same routes were often played year after year and attendance at the shows became an annual ritual. A few, including Henry L. Brunk, Skeeter Kell, J. Doug Morgan and Warren Noble, had their repertoire outfits on the rails. This car carried the Roberson Players, owned by George and Claudia Robserson, at least one season. *Photograph, 1921, Thomas P. Parkinson Collection, Circus World Museum.*

Sam and Donna Houston assembled a two-car attraction in Baldwin Park, California, utilizing a former 1945 Arthur Bros. Circus 80-foot boxcar and a passenger car that had once served as the Arthur Bros. advertising car. The Arthur stock car previously was with the Conklin shows in Canada and may have been built by Warran. A walk-through show on wheels, the attractions included a midget Japanese submarine, a primate reputed to be a gorilla and several small cages of animals. The opposite side of the boxcar had the word "GORILLA" painted on it in similarly large letters. The Houstons' outfit was routed east to El Paso, Texas, and then into Mexico and obscurity. *Photographs by Charles Puck, circa 1946, Gift, Charles Puck Collection, Circus World Museum.*

Howard Y. Bary had an interesting career as a promoter and agent for circuses and other forms of attractions. For the season of 1938 he leased the big Hagenbeck-Wallace Circus from the Ringling interests. In 1950 he conceived of the idea of a touring zoo on wheels. He purchased two baggage cars and a diner from the Santa Fe Railroad and transformed them into a walk-through operation at Peru, Indiana. The attraction opened at the Canadian National Exhibition of 1951. It was titled the British American Zoo, possibly because of the Toronto opening. The features included several chimpanzees, a pigmy hippo, a baby camel and a baby elephant. Rising railroad rates forced Bary to park the train and open a landed zoo. The Bary train was last known to be in a Reading, Pennsylvania, scrap yard. *Photograph by Art Stensvad, undated, circa 1954, Gift, Bill Green Collection, Circus World Museum.*

One of the earliest views of a carnival train shows the Gaskill Carnival Company after a railroad wreck. Show owner Frank W. Gaskill of Alliance, Ohio, has generally been credited with being the first showman who brought together all of the elements that defined a carnival and then toured it for an entire season. Several makes of flat cars were in the Gaskill train. Some, like the car in the middle, were owned by the show and painted with the title "Gaskill Carnival Company." Others were 60-footers leased from the Venice Transportation Company. The derailed Gaskill flat carried the portable steam engines that powered the show's electrical generators, possibly contained within the two wagons on the same car. *Photograph, June 23, 1905, Atchison, Kansas, Fred D. Pfening, Jr. Collection.*

The Southern Iron and Equipment Company furnished several styles of cars, including this 60-foot, 80,000-pound capacity boxcar, to K. G. Barkoot World's Greatest Shows. Known more for the buying and selling of cars than their construction, this car nonetheless carries an inscription crediting its manufacture to SI&E. Carnival trains included boxcars for the transport of supplies, spare parts and other essentials that were difficult to acquire once the show was en route. In an era when brand name litigation was less common, it apparently did not matter to Syrian-born Khalie George Barkoot that the Ringling brothers had commenced the use of the slogan "World's Greatest Shows" in 1891, years before he went on the road with his own carnival company. *Photograph, circa 1910, Atlanta, Georgia, Ray W. Buhrmaster Collection.*

Barkoot also purchased sleepers for his train from the Southern Iron & Equipment Company. Traveling shows generally both fed and housed their employees. Food service was provided in a cookhouse tent erected on the show grounds. Some of the larger shows had dining cars in their train, or the more frequently encountered "pie car," where snack foods and drinks were available. After the show was unloaded and the midway erected, workingmen frequently slept inside tents or under and inside wagons on the show grounds. Because carnivals generally moved between communities only once per week, their trains put on many fewer miles in a year than a circus or wild west aggregation, which moved daily. *Photograph, August 24, 1910, Atlanta, Georgia, Ray W. Buhrmaster Collection.*

The Venice Transportation Company of St. Louis, Missouri, leased flat cars, and in some cases, stock cars, to carnivals, circuses, wild west shows and other non-show users. Their cars were generally manufactured by conventional car builders. This 50 or 60-foot, 50,000-pound capacity flat was made by the Terre Haute Car and Manufacturing Company, Terre Haute, Indiana, a plant that later became part of the American Car & Foundry Company. This flat car had an unusual triple truss rod arrangement that may represent a transitional design to longer flat cars. For showmen with inadequate capital to buy their own vehicles, leased cars provided a means by which they could take to the road with less money invested. Other shows that owned their own cars might have leased a few in a pinch, such as for short-term expansion or to replace cars lost or damaged in a wreck. *Photograph, circa 1894, St. Charles, Missouri, courtesy ACF Industries and Frank M. Ellington.*

The Greater United Shows was active at least two years, 1911 and 1912. A 1911 contract with the Louisville & Nashville Railroad Company called for the road to furnish three coaches for show use and to also haul the nine flats, two Arms Palace Horse Car Company cars, two stock cars and four coaches owned by the carnival. Seen in this view are three Arms cars, two stocks, about ten flats and five coaches, or a total of twenty cars. The L&N charged one dollar per day to store the show's cars and assessed a fee of $487.50 to move the show from Louisville, Kentucky, to Nashville, Tennessee. Features transported on the train included Hargraves' Old Fashioned One Ring Circus, the mechanical Electric City, Princess Maxine (the Mule with a Human Brain), Toddles the elephant and a Big Eli Ferris wheel. It was a complete midway on wheels. *Photograph, circa 1911, Oshkosh, Wisconsin, Circus World Museum.*

One of the most remarkable photographs in carnival history is this panoramic image of K. G. Barkoot World's Greatest Shows entire train. Nineteen cars were stretched out between the Pennsylvania Railroad's steam locomotive and four-wheel caboose, including four boxcars, one stock car, nine flat cars and five sleepers. To have an odd number of cars was unusual as show car rates were generally established in multiples of five cars. Carnivals did not utilize advertising cars as their weekly moves and local sponsorships did not mandate as aggressive an advance as mounted by circuses and wild west concerns. The locomotive and caboose confirm the location as being on Pennsylvania Railroad trackage, but the line did not take a direct route between the two cities identified on the print as the location. *Panorama photograph by C. E. Scarlett, September 14, 1913, between Mt. Vernon and Newark, Ohio, Howard C. Tibbals Collection.*

Barkoot bought two surplus Ringling Bros. flat cars in early 1912. Several of the flats in the consist, with smooth sides, have a Ringling look to them and may be the ones from the Baraboo, Wisconsin, brothers' operation. The remaining flats have some characteristics of Mt. Vernon-built cars and may have originated with that source. Loaded on the flats were the show's office and baggage wagons, wagons that unfolded and became show fronts (covered with canvas), a bandwagon (with pipe handrail and seats on top) and others that carried mechanical rides, such as a carousel, a pleasure wheel and swings. The show title was nicely painted with shaded lettering on each car. *Panorama photograph by C. E. Scarlett, September 14, 1913, between Mt. Vernon and Newark, Ohio, Howard C. Tibbals Collection.*

The lone stock car in the Barkoot train, located between the flat cars and the boxcars, was formerly a Burton Stock Car Company vehicle. Burton, like the Arms Palace Horse Car Company, leased stock cars to shows and other concerns that needed to transport stock in a humane manner across the country. The show carried only enough horses to unload the train and perhaps pull a few wagons in a street parade. Other teams and trucks were hired locally to pull wagons to and from the show lot. In addition to supplies and spare parts, the boxcars may have transported show equipment that was "gillied" by labor and knockdown wagons between the train and the show grounds. The boxcar immediately after the locomotive tender may be a system car supplied by the railroad. *Panorama photograph by C. E. Scarlett, September 14, 1913, between Mt. Vernon and Newark, Ohio, Howard C. Tibbals Collection.*

The first carnival owner known to have acquired steel frame stock or flat cars was Johnny J. Jones. It is fairly certain that he bought a Standard Steel Car Company flat car in 1911, but then turned to the Warren Tank Car Company the following year and commenced the assembling of the trains that he proudly hailed as the "Jones Flyer." His Exposition was the first carnival to purchase and use a large fleet of steel cars, with the great majority of them made by Warren. This faded loading scene is the only known 1910s photograph showing Jones's flat cars. It is believed that the Warren design used from 1912 onwards was the same as the cars for which they were known in the 1920s and 1930s. *Card photograph, 1915, Uniontown, Pennsylvania, Circus World Museum.*

Johnny J. Jones was another showman who purchased sleeping cars from the Southern Iron & Equipment Company. The dual open platforms of the "Caroline" suggest a vintage vehicle and perhaps use as a railroad business or inspection car. The wider windows in the center of the car were possibly replacements for the smaller windows like those towards the ends. While shows often retained their stock, box and flat cars for years, even decades, it appears that the sleeping and private cars were subject to more frequent turnover. *Photograph, undated, Atlanta, Georgia, California State Railroad Museum.*

C. W. Parker of Abilene, and later Leavenworth, Kansas, was America's prolific builder of carnivals and mechanical rides. Parker would buy one of everything and then set about to determine how he could fabricate it in his own shop. Typically he succeeded, but with some loss of artistic merit or technology. His men constructed the wood flat car shown here, along with the Parker Carry-Us-All merry-go-round and the three wagons that hauled it. Parker and Charles Andress, a long time circus man, placed two identical carousels on circuses in 1915 and 1916 to demonstrate their portability. This is the outfit that traveled with Fred Buchanan's Yankee Robinson Circus. Parker fabricated many flat cars that carried his own shows and that of other carnival "sheiks," as the owners were sometimes termed. *Photograph by L. Moxie Hanley, 1916, probably Granger, Iowa, Circus World Museum.*

Although it was mostly a flat car operation and destined to be an industry leader, Rubin Gruberg's Rubin & Cherry Shows still gillied some equipment from the train to the lot in 1917. More items could be packed into a boxcar than could be loaded on a flat car of the same length, but an enormous demand was placed on human labor to both load and unload the materials. Trunks, bundles of canvas, planks and innumerable other items had to be handled twice during each operation, making it a costly and time-consuming practice. As shows prospered, they typically converted from a gilly to flat car operation. The Rubin & Cherry car on the right had the lines of a system milk or express baggage car. *Photograph, 1917, Albert Conover Collection.*

Rubin & Cherry acquired this fine arch window dining car from Southern Iron and Equipment Company in March 1921. Cars such as this one generally served to offer meals when the show was in transit, or drinks, sandwiches and desserts like pie when personnel were not needed on the grounds. Carnivals would adapt and update wood cars with steel sheathing and contemporary features to make them acceptable to the railroads of the time. *Photograph, 1921, Atlanta, Georgia, Ray W. Buhrmaster Collection.*

Harry G. Melville was a carnival owner and manager. He married the widow of Nat Reiss and thereby came into the ownership of the Nat Reiss Shows, a significant railroad carnival. To satisfy the need for additional show flats in the early 1920s, Melville arranged for an unidentified Illinois builder to make both 60 to 63-foot, 80,000-pound capacity wood cars and also 70-foot steel cars of the same load rating. Melville claimed to have sold several dozen of them to a variety of carnivals. Four identified Melville flat car buyers were Dodson's World's Fair Shows, Snapp Bros. Shows, Rubin & Cherry Exposition and the Foley & Burk Combined Shows. The last named carnival purchased four Melville flats in 1921 and three of them are shown here. They survived at least into the 1930s. The end of a former Buck Jones Wild West Warren-built flat was on the left. *Photograph, undated, California State Railroad Museum.*

Between 1920 and 1924 the Mt. Vernon Car Manufacturing Company designed and fabricated two different styles of flat cars with straight profile sides. This one was their second attempt at a flat car that mimicked the Warren design. Several of these vehicles were in use over a decade later on the Beckmann & Gerety Shows. Despite the cars being fitted with a support truss under the draft or center sills, car number 25 exhibited a sway-backed condition. This was highly unusual for a steel car and probably indicated a design deficiency. Just a few show proprietors favored this style of car and only a limited number were built. In spite of their apparent shortcomings, a Mt. Vernon car of this design was with the Mighty Sheesley Shows and later Cetlin & Wilson Shows until the 1960s. Another toured with the World of Mirth carnival until 1963 and still survives today. *Photograph, July 26, 1937, Robert DeVoe Collection.*

By April 1921, the Mt. Vernon Car Manufacturing Company fabricated the first of its successful fish belly style flat cars for a circus. A 1925 Mt. Vernon advertisement illustrated perhaps the first such car sold to a railroad carnival, having the L. J. Heth Shows title on it. Similar 70-foot Mt. Vernon flats were supplied to the Hagenbeck-Wallace Circus in the early 1920s. Mt. Vernon flats of 72-foot length went to the John Robinson Circus for 1928. Cars from both sources ended up in the Hagenbeck-Wallace Circus train of the late 1930s. Parts of it were sold to the Art Lewis Shows, explaining the presence of these Mt. Vernon cars in the Lewis train. *Photograph, June 23, 1940, Newport, Rhode Island, Fred Heatley Collection.*

The operational dates of the W. E. Groff Shows have not been determined. The entire Groff show may have been outfitted in the yard of C. W. Parker. The steel outside sills on these flat cars suggested that it toured in the late 1910s or early 1920s. The term "semi-steel" was sometimes applied to these cars because they incorporated both rolled steel members and wood in their framing. A close examination will reveal heavy wood timbers used for the end sills, while the outside sills were steel. Truss rods were used to handle the tension loads in the car design. The wagons with carvings were C. W. Parker-built show front wagons with fold out panels. The laced structural elements on the far right were the upright supports for a Big Eli make pleasure (Ferris) wheel. *Print from original negative, undated, Circus World Museum.*

Carnivals used the same methods devised by circuses decades earlier for the loading and unloading of their flat cars. Men, horses and simple machines accomplished the task with a minimum of energy and time. Here a poler steers a canvas covered wagon to the runs on the Morris and Castle Shows, the wagon propelled by the team of baggage horses that walked beside the flats. The canvas wagon covers protected the decorative elements on show front and parade wagons from weather, vandals and locomotive smoke. Infrequently sparks from the locomotive exhaust ignited a fire in them that would have to be extinguished while the train was en route to the next destination. *Photograph, circa 1928, Fred D. Pfening, Jr. Collection.*

In 1929, the Southern Pacific Railroad shops in Oakland, California, fabricated ten or more 60-foot flat cars for the Foley & Burk Shows, a largely California railroad show. They always remained Foley & Burk carnival property, with the exception of one that became part of the 1945 Arthur Bros. Circus train. Different reports have been made about the origin of the cars, but it appears that they were assembled from other system cars of an enclosed style, perhaps box or furniture cars. *Photograph, 1941, California State Railroad Museum.*

A device called a "snatch block" by showmen, consisting of a special pulley with a hook attached to the housing, was used to help load this heavy Model Shows of America electrical department wagon. It can be seen attached to the right front bullring on the wagon. The snatch block, used in conjunction with the pull-up rope, halved the force necessary to raise the wagon from the ground to the top deck of the car but doubled the distance that the pull-up team walked. The Warren Tank Car Company fabricated this flat car for the Model Shows of America, Rubin Gruberg's number two carnival, in July 1927. *Photograph by Crosby, October 4, 1931, Shelby, North Carolina, Howard C. Tibbals Collection.*

One section of the Johnny J. Jones Exposition was brought into town behind a fine Southern Railroad Class Ms-4 locomotive, number 4825. It was built at the Richmond, Virginia, works of the American Locomotive Company in 1923. During the steam era, railroads assigned freight engines like this Mikado style (2-8-2 wheel arrangement) engine to haul show trains, much as they would their own regularly scheduled freight trains. Speed was not paramount in moving the carnival from one location to another. Like large circuses, carnivals in excess of thirty cars or so were typically hauled in separate sections by the railroad. The smoke discharged by steam locomotives caused showmen to generally place their passenger cars at the rear of the train, giving time for the smoke to dissipate before the cars rolled through it. Unfortunately, it also meant that the sleepers experienced the greatest amount of slack take-up when the train started, stopped or braked, giving the occupants an earthquake-proportion jolt. *Photograph by Crosby, 1932, Shelby, North Carolina, Howard C. Tibbals Collection.*

The Johnny J. Jones Exposition was the top carnival for a number of years and made a flashy appearance both on the lot and on the rails. There are two 70 or 72-foot Warren-built flat cars on the right coupled to the single 60-foot Standard Steel Car Company flat owned by the show. The Warrens had a steel channel truss system beneath the draft sills, with lateral bracing extending over to the side frames. The construction was typical of Warren flats supplied to carnivals and possibly other shows until the late 1920s. The presence of different length flat cars made loading something of a challenge for the show trainmaster. He would have to arrange the wagons in a loading order so that they would all fit, yet also meet the various time schedule needs of the personnel and show. *Photograph by Crosby, 1932, Shelby, North Carolina, Fred D. Pfening, Jr. Collection.*

By the time this photograph was taken, the Johnny J. Jones Exposition was in the hands of E. Lawrence Phillips, who brought new life into the show during the depths of the Depression. Phillips began to expand the carnival and lacking adequate flats, he leased several system flat cars to carry some of the show's wagons and trucks. Three of them can be seen in the right center of the image. In later years the show would have two former whale show cars, converted into flats, to haul wagons. Some of the Warren flats seen here may have been among the earliest steel cars fabricated for traveling show use. *Photograph, 1938, Joe Pearl Collection, courtesy Jim Parker.*

The 40-car United Shows of America journeyed across the Pacific Northwest via the electrified mainline of the Chicago, Milwaukee, St. Paul and Pacific Railroad. The show train was hauled in one unit, with Milwaukee Road box-cab electric locomotives of the EF-1 class cut into the consist at an appropriate location as helpers. Another similar pair of engines, designated as an A-B set, was at the head of the train. These powerful engines (3340 horsepower per pair) were built by General Electric at Schenectady, New York, in 1916 and stayed in service for decades. Flat car number 38 was a 61 or 62-foot long vehicle made by the Haffner-Thrall Car Company of Chicago, Illinois, in the early 1920s. There were four system railroad flat cars leased for this move, placed immediately ahead of the coaches. *Photograph by C. Owen Smithers, July 21, 1936, near Butte, Montana, Rolland L. Lohmar Scrapbook, Gift, James Elliott, Circus World Museum, with permission of Smithers Studio.*

The flats towards the end of the first section and in the second section of the United Shows of America train were Warren-built flat cars. Whether it was because of price or design features, Warren received the majority of car orders from traveling shows in the 1920s and 1930s. Latter day showmen indicated that Mt. Vernon cars required more maintenance and did not endure as long in railroad service. Following the flats were the show sleepers and a Milwaukee Road caboose. *Photograph by C. Owen Smithers, July 21, 1936, near Butte, Montana, Rolland L. Lohmar Scrapbook, Gift, James Elliott, Circus World Museum, with permission of Smithers Studio.*

The differences between the two principal cars in this view illustrate the design evolution that took place over about one decade. The car on the left was one of the 60-foot steel-frame stocks made by the Standard Steel Car Company to their 1911 design. The stock or boxcar on the right was a 70 or 72-foot steel car of the style built by the Warren Tank Car Company in the 1920s. Some shows simply replaced wood cars with steel on a one-for-one basis, thereby gaining about an additional ten feet of loading capacity in the conversion. *Photograph by Gene Baxter, 1938, Gift, Gene Baxter, Circus World Museum.*

Hennies Bros. Shows acquired this gigantic 80-foot long boxcar sometime before the 1940 tour. It had several Warren Tank Car Company design hallmarks, but the attribution has yet to be confirmed. The Warren-like features included the rolled steel channel end sill with attached push pockets and the solid plate car body ends with two vertical members stiffening it. The car remained with the show train after it became the Amusement Corporation of America and later Olson Shows. Perhaps cars such as this one anticipated the jumbo-sized "Hi-Cube" boxcars fabricated decades later for system railroad use. *Photograph by William Koford, 1942, Albert Conover Collection.*

Among the heaviest wagons on any traveling show were the generator or light plant wagons. Rubin & Cherry Exposition generator number 2, housed in a wagon built by the Springfield Wagon & Trailer Company, was carefully steered, or "poled" in show language, across a flat to the runs. Special care was necessary to assure that the pneumatic tires did not contact the inside face of the flat car gunwales. The stiffness of the rubber would cause the front undergear to rapidly turn in the direction of the contact, throwing or knocking the poler off his feet. Trainmaster McLane stood ready to throw a chock in front of a wheel in the event that the wagon went out of control. The snubber post man wrapped his rope around the dual snubber posts, ready to retard the wagon during its descent of the runs. This 100,000-pound capacity flat car was made by the Warren Tank Car Company in August 1928 and was likely 72 feet long. *Photograph by Jack Dadswell, 1941, Rolland L. Lohmar Scrapbook, Gift, James Elliott, Circus World Museum.*

The porters that serviced show sleepers were almost exclusively African-Americans. Here's the crew that tended to the needs of the occupants on the Rubin & Cherry Exposition train in 1941. They're seated on the platform of the observation car that trailed the train and was typically occupied by the show's owner or general manager. Head Porter Willis Tolliver is the man on the left, and with him are Willie Sutton, Frankie Bell, "Pee Wee," Freddie Brown and Lonnie Wilson. *Photograph by Yucho Chow, 1941, Vancouver, British Columbia, Canada, Rolland L. Lohmar Scrapbook, Gift, James Elliott, Circus World Museum.*

The World of Mirth never supplied sleeping or transportation accommodations for all of its staff and working people. That explains why there were only three sleepers in the show train. To the right was a stock car and beyond that were some of the show's flats, including both Mt. Vernons and Warrens. Though the World of Mirth had fewer sleepers than other carnivals of its class, it was still a major midway with a strong route. *Photograph by Gene Baxter, circa 1942, Robert S. MacDougall Collection.*

The Endy Bros. Shows, owned and managed by Dave B. Endy from 1945 to 1950 inclusive, bought the Art Lewis Shows train. The purchase included the Mt. Vernon flats previously with Hagenbeck-Wallace. The show had a modified agricultural tractor to haul wagons and also acquired an industrial tractor to replace the pullover team. Endy's private car, the "Joan B.," was immediately behind wagon number 188, with show sleepers behind it. *Photograph from an Endy Bros. Shows Christmas card, circa 1947, Joseph Brislin Collection, Gift, Michael D. Sporrer, Circus World Museum.*

The Haffner-Thrall Car Company of Chicago Heights, Illinois, was contracted to build several flats for the Hennies Bros. Shows. Six cars were ordered in late 1945, but they may not have been delivered until April 1947 because of post-war material shortages. The flats were not painted with the show's identification other than "HBX" until after they were received and placed in service. This Haffner-Thrall design had a top and bottom flange on the sides and six vertical stiffeners. The cars were rated at 100,000-pounds capacity and were probably 72 feet long. The Hennies show, and its successors, the Amusement Corporation of America and the Olson Shows, utilized other flats of several different fish belly configurations that may have been rebuilds or revisions of this design, or entirely new cars. It's likely that they all came from the Haffner-Thrall shop. *Photograph, circa 1947, Howard C. Tibbals Collection.*

The Haffner-Thrall Car Company designed another style of flat that saw use on Al Wagner's big 50-car Cavalcade of Amusements, "The Nation's Greatest Show," in the early 1950s. Similar to a dozen flats supplied by Haffner-Thrall to Ringling Bros. and Barnum & Bailey Combined Shows in 1949 and 1955, they were later acquired by the Royal American Shows following the closure of the Cavalcade operation. The Haffner-Thrall flats were the four with smooth sides and the fish belly drop in the center. Haffner-Thrall was active as a show car builder from the early 1920s to the mid-1950s, and conducts business today as the Thrall Car Manufacturing Company. *Photograph, June 1953, Robert S. MacDougall Collection.*

There were at least six different makes of flat cars in the 1950s Cetlin & Wilson Shows train. Flat cars numbered 139 (right) and 138 (center) had an uncertain pedigree but appear to be upgrades of older semi-steel cars. The car on the far left was one of four that were originally Al G. Barnes and Sells-Floto Combined Shows stock cars through 1938. They were altered into flat cars by Ringling Bros. and Barnum & Bailey Combined Shows during the 1941 season and sold to others in the late 1940s. The Endy Bros. Shows and the World of Mirth also had stock cars that were adapted into flat cars. *Photograph, 1950, Durand, Michigan, Fred D. Pfening, Jr. Collection.*

The Cetlin & Wilson Shows had a very eclectic group of cars in their train. The "Roanoke" was a former Arms Palace Horse Car Company stock car that had been converted for show use with end-loading doors. The car was like others that had been built for Arms by the Pullman Company in the early 1910s. It is likely that all of the stalls and partitioning that once divided the interior were removed in favor of bunks for working men or clear space for show equipment. *Photograph by Joseph T. Bradbury, October 1952, Atlanta, Georgia, courtesy Paul Horsman.*

The two boys on bikes got a special treat when the Royal American Shows train came into town on the Rock Island Railroad. Encounters like this set many juvenile imaginations into overdrive. Following the steam locomotive with its distinctive tender tank were two stock cars and numerous Warren flats. Though the Royal American Shows train is generally remembered for its aluminum-painted cars, when this photograph was taken the flats were orange and the wagons were aluminum. Piloted by Carl J. Sedlmayr, Sr., the show established a reputation as the best and mightiest in the business, a position that it would hold for decades. It played the Minnesota State Fair for sixty-two years, a record never equaled by any other traveling midway. *Photograph by Gene Baxter, 1938, Gift, Gene Baxter, Circus World Museum.*

Steel frame stock cars like this one built by the Standard Steel Car Company were sided with wood. The 60-foot long Standard Steel stock cars had fewer side truss panels (thirteen) than 70 and 72-foot Warren-built stocks (fifteen). On Warren cars, the vertical and diagonal lacing channels forming the truss opened outwards, while on Standard cars they faced the inside. In later years, when the cars hauled supplies and equipment instead of animals, the wood was typically replaced with steel sheeting. By the time it ceased rail operations, Royal American Shows had bought cars from several other carnivals, retaining the best of each and selling off the lesser cars to other operations. By that means it was able to maintain an excellent fleet of cars while actually making money peddling the older cars. *Photograph, circa 1944, Circus World Museum.*

This unusual combination car was with the 1945 Arthur Bros. Circus before being acquired by the Royal American Shows. Why it was termed the "Flying Squadron" is unknown. That phrase, originally simply "squadron," was used towards the beginning of the 20th century by circuses to designate the first train section to depart for the next city to be visited. It carried the cookhouse and other essentials that were necessary to initiate show operations in the community. *Photograph, circa 1947, California State Railroad Museum.*

A few carnivals employed motor trucks for the movement of their wagons as early as the mid-1910s. Agricultural and industrial tractors also served in loading and pulling service, but the workhorse of the carnival was the crawler-type tractor with tracks, particularly the Caterpillar tractor. The Royal American Shows sometimes utilized a model D-6 Caterpillar with an attached steel cable spool to load wagons. As soon as the wagon was on the flat car deck, it was pulled into its final position on the flats by the agricultural tractor ahead of the Caterpillar. *Photograph by Jim Dugan, May 15, 1949, Memphis, Tennessee, permission granted by Caterpillar Inc., Howard C. Tibbals Collection.*

There were at least thirteen sleepers coupled in front of Carl J. Sedlmayr Sr.'s private car number 60. The first one, car number 50, was actually the private car of his son, C.J. Sedlmayr, Jr., and his family. The observation had previously served on the Rubin & Cherry Exposition and may have been Rubin Gruberg's own private car, the "Montgomery," about 1930. The best-remembered decorative scheme of these cars included red letter boards and lower sides, yellow between the windows and black trim around them, all topped by aluminum roofs. They made an imposing sight on any railroad siding, with generators idling to provide electric power to lights and other facilities on board. *Photograph, undated, Howard C. Tibbals Collection.*

Despite the brilliant paint colors of the wagons and train cars, the loading of a carnival at night presented additional challenges to the crew. To light the way in dimly lit railroad sidings and yards, the train crew placed light standards at periodic places along the cut of flats to be loaded. Each flat was wired with 110-volt outlets that were then connected together from car to car. The wagon-mounted train light plant, parked near the cars, supplied the power to illuminate the bulbs. A truck tractor has just pulled one of the massive Royal American Shows generator wagons over the flats towards the end of the train. Another cut of loaded Royal cars sat on the adjacent track. *Photograph by Orin Copple King, September 1965, Topeka, Kansas, courtesy Kinder von RAS.*

Road locomotives hauled carnival trains between communities, but diesel-electric switch engines arranged the various cuts of cars for unloading after the show arrived. A Rock Island Railroad switcher built by General Motors Electro-Motive Division shifted the "gas cut," meaning the flats with internal combustion powered tractors and trucks, in preparation for the unloading of the show. The Haffner-Thrall Car Company manufactured all of the flat cars shown here for the Ringling Bros. and Barnum & Bailey Combined Shows. Ten were fabricated in 1949 and two, with a slightly different design, in 1955. They went to the Royal American Shows about 1961, after the circus abandoned its traditional flat car circus operation in 1956. *Photograph by Orin Copple King, September 1965, Topeka, Kansas, courtesy Kinder von RAS.*

The mammoth winter quarters of the Royal American Shows included extensive trackage for the storage and repair of the world's largest carnival train. Visible in this aerial view are two stock or boxcars, 66 flats and 29 sleepers. Nine former U. S. Army troop train kitchen cars and two retired boxcars were also on the ground, used for the storage of wardrobe and other show properties. This 40-acre site was first occupied in 1972, the show having previously prepared for the road on the Tampa fairgrounds and elsewhere. *Photograph, May 30, 1976, Tampa, Florida, courtesy Selbypic, Inc.*

The Royal American Shows train reached a maximum size of 90 cars in 1971. Here is just one section of the train moving on the Burlington Northern Railroad, pulled by two Electro-Motive Division diesel-electric road locomotives, a GP 20 and a GP 30. Immediately after the locomotives is a single Warren flat. The twelve Thrall-built flat cars and almost another twenty Warrens followed, with some of the show sleepers trailing behind. With all of the railroad cars and wagons decorated by the show's veteran show painter Bobby Wicks, it made an unforgettable sight passing through the verdant countryside. *Photograph by Bernard Corbin, 1980, near Red Oak, Iowa, courtesy Hol Wagner, Robert S. MacDougall Collection.*

The James E. Strates Show was organized as the motorized Southern Tier Shows in 1923 and converted to rails in 1933. Through the years the Strates train included both wood and steel flats. The cut of cars in the foreground included both Mt. Vernon and Warren-built steel flats. The Strates organization also owned the last surviving Keith Railway Equipment Company flat cars, which had been built in 1922 for the Sells-Floto Circus. They were used on both the Strates show and other major railroad carnivals affiliated with the Strates operation. *Photograph, 1957, Plainfield, New Jersey, Circus World Museum.*

The James E. Strates Shows owns and operates the only carnival train in the United States today. By 1968 the firm commenced to upgrade the show train with newer 85-foot long piggyback-type flat cars. They replaced the three to four-decades old Mt. Vernon, Keith and Warren flat cars, which were retired and scrapped. One Warren flat remains in service today, used as part of the Strates show's unique loading ramp system. Shorter, wagon-like vehicles have also been replaced by conventional semi-trailer trucks whenever possible. Railroad regulations prohibit show personnel from riding on the train when it is underway, causing the sleepers to be used only after they have been spotted on a siding. Despite the challenges of fewer railroad sidings, increasing railroad and insurance restrictions, and other challenges, the Strates family still perceives value from the operation of their unique show train. The Strates train was loaded and a razorback walked off to the next engagement. *Photograph by Gene Baxter, 1970, Albany, New York, Gift, Gene Baxter, Circus World Museum.*

MORE TITLES FROM ICONOGRAFIX:

AMERICAN CULTURE

AUTOMOTIVE

BUSES

EMERGENCY VEHICLES

RACING

RAILWAYS

TRUCKS

TRACTORS & CONSTRUCTION EQUIPMENT

All Iconografix books are available from direct mail specialty book dealers and bookstores worldwide, or can be ordered from the publisher. For book trade and distribution information or to add your name to our mailing list and receive a **FREE CATALOG** contact:

Iconografix, PO Box 446, Hudson, Wisconsin, 54016   Telephone: (715) 381-9755, (800) 289-3504 (USA), Fax: (715) 381-9756

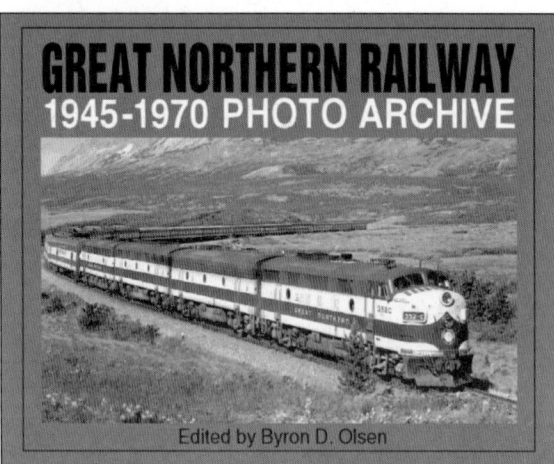
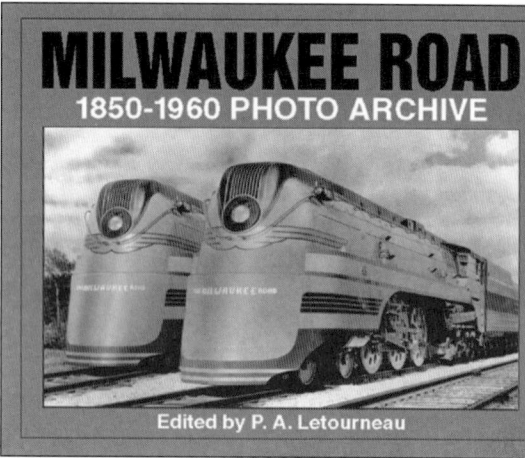
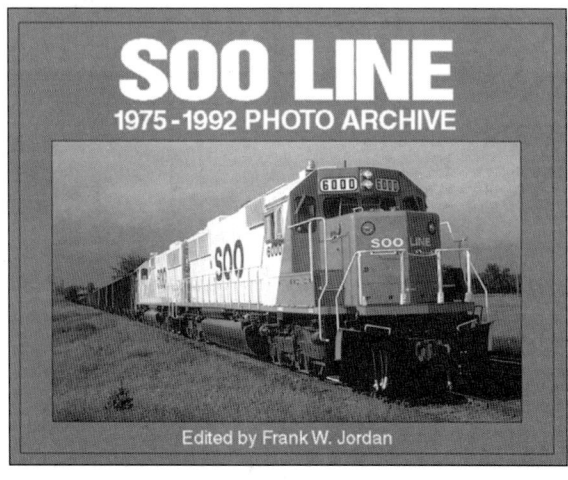